J-WOND

Judah Jensen

In this imagining of Judah's brave journey defying the odds with the strong love of his family. The lion accompanying Judah throughout the story represents the 'Lion of Judah' (never leaving Judah's side, showing God's constant vigil) and the reactions of the character mirror the emotions/atmosphere of the different stages throughout the journey.

J-WONDER

Judah Jensen

Sometimes people think of life as a journey, and every journey has a beginning.

My beginning has been very different from how a lot of people imagine things will go.

There was an emergency - lots of doctors were around.

None were sure why things weren't happening as expected.

It was a massive worry.

Luckily a doctor from Birmingham came to save the day.

The staff in the hospital had to watch me very closely - I was teaching them something new every day. I moved around to different hospitals

- here I'm in the NICU in Birmingham.

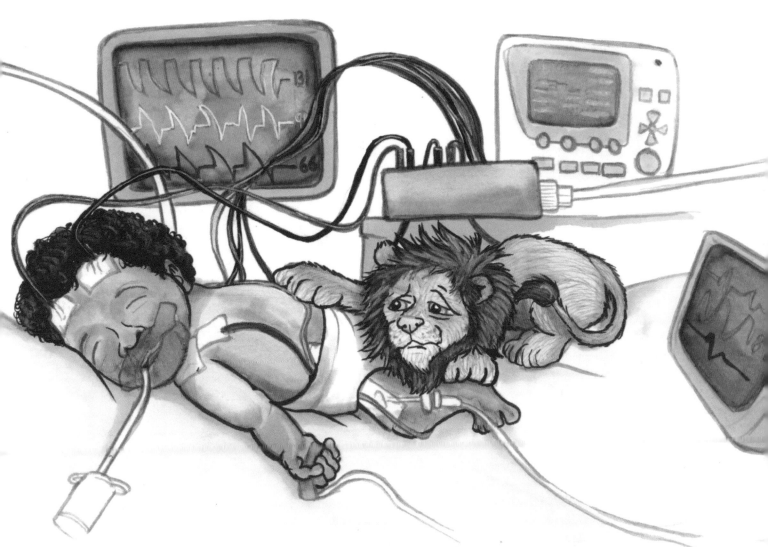

As you can see, I'm not alone - the love of those looking out for me seems to give my tiny body strength.

Of course I'm not the only one beginnning their journey along an unfamiliar and unexpected path.

New and unfamiliar things are scary for anyone, any support and guidance is comforting.

The peace that you get from knowing someone is looking out for you and sharing your journey makes you feel even stronger.

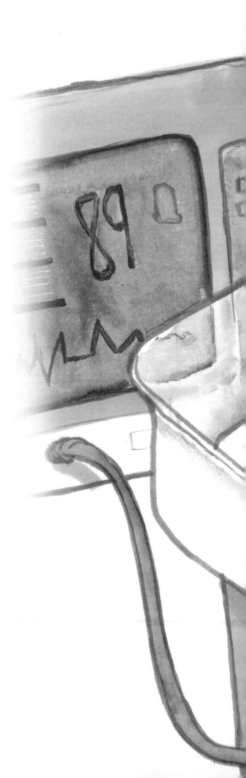

Sometimes journeys take unexpected and unhelpful twists and when I was ill with covid things were really hard.

Again, the support and love were there to help me through this tricky phase.

My transfer to Ward 9 - a ward fit for a King!

A little time to take stock, enjoy some different new technology , the sort that's there to entertain!

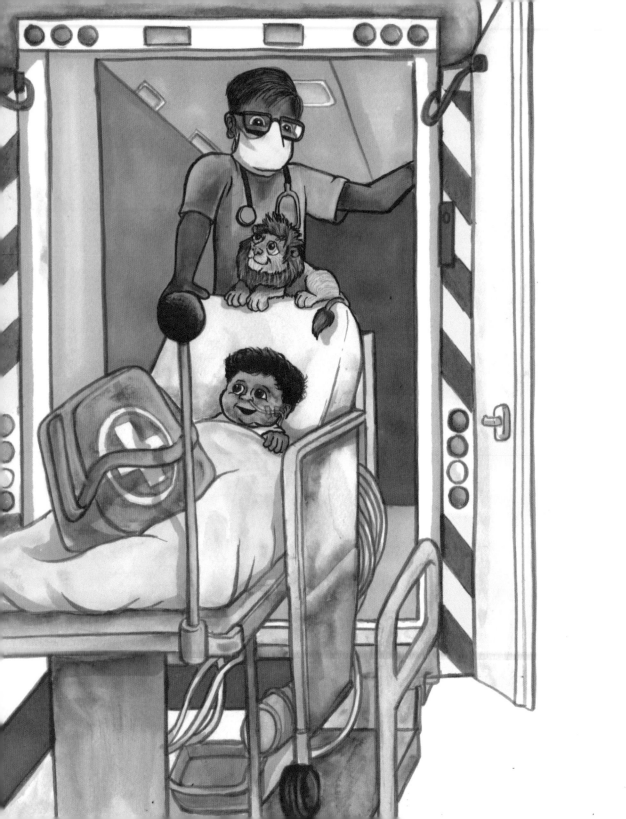

Now another journey within a journey.

My Transport down to Great Ormond Street Hospital in London.
Travelling in style!

A huge event - doctors, surgeons and other staff assisting my journey in a massive way.

Alarming and unnerving for everyone (not so much for me, I was asleep all the way through!)

I could be calm knowing that I was being cared and watched out for.

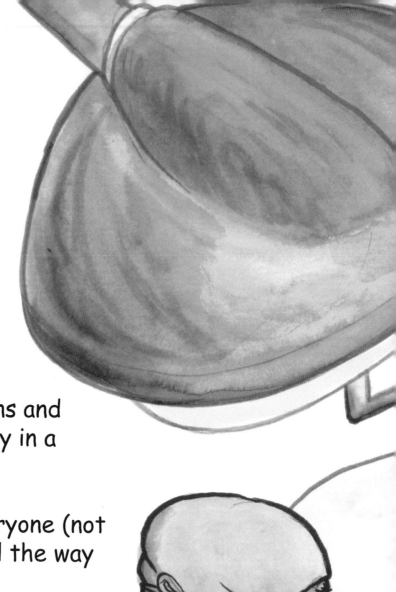

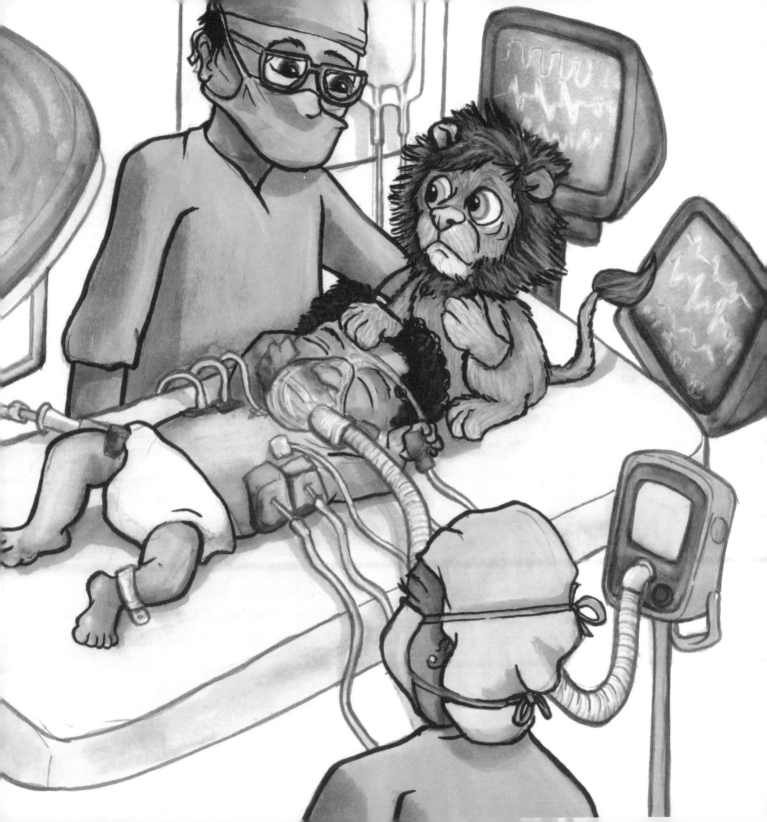

Everyone's journey is different, some go the way that people hope and expect they will, some end way too soon.

There was a time when it seemed that my journey could be nearly over. No one knew what to expect.

Then, all of a sudden, it was all systems go!

I found a place in Bear ward where I could amaze everyone by showing off all the wonderful things I could do.

The love of those caring and watching over me again being the support that I need.

I wonder how it felt to see me doing all of these things for the first time?

The fight that I have inside me, vanquishing those things that appear and try to scupper and wreck my journey, grows stronger every day.

Knowing that there's always someone there is the strengthener that makes me J- WONDER!

This part of my journey has been 7 months long and I'm proud of where I've got to so far with help from all this wonderful team.

I've made my start, the journey goes on.

What will I do?

Where will I go next?

I don't know, none of us do.

One thing is for sure though, I'm not travelling alone and I'll be loved all the way.

Printed in Great Britain
by Amazon